THIS BOOK BELONGS TO:

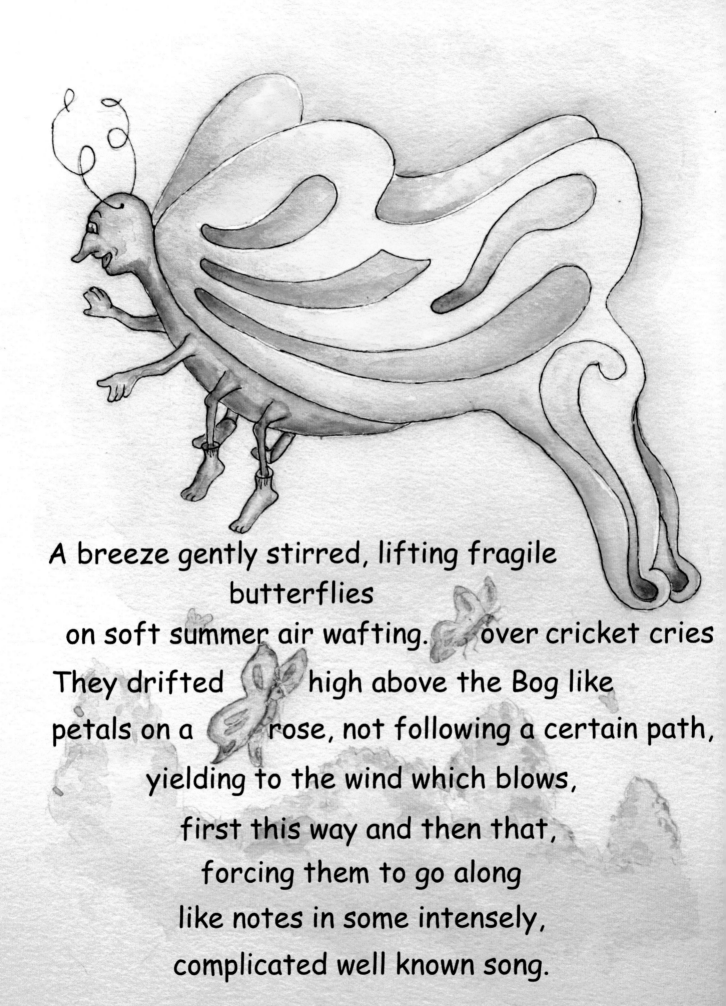

A breeze gently stirred, lifting fragile
butterflies
on soft summer air wafting.   over cricket cries
They drifted   high above the Bog like
petals on a   rose, not following a certain path,
yielding to the wind which blows,
first this way and then that,
forcing them to go along
like notes in some intensely,
complicated well known song.

Hartlie watched from down below
as they danced before the breeze,
wishing he could take off too
as they did with such ease.

He watched them so intently that he very
nearly trod on
Wooly Worm who crawled so slow across the
soft green sod.

"My gosh! I didn't see you!" Hartlie gasped
with great surprise as his brown boot came
within an inch of Wooly's nose and eyes.

"Oh...it's ok...I'm used to it," Wooly said all
down and out,
"I stay bumped and bruised...black and blue
that's what my life's about."

"Why so glum my fuzzy
friend?
It seems you should be glad,

thankful that my shoe missed
you,
instead you seem so sad."

"My life is not the best there is,"
he sighed and then he squirmed,
further down the path of life
all brown and wooly wormed.

"I'm boring...and I'm ugly,
that's why I have no friends,
that's how the cookie crumbles,
that's how my story ends.

Oh me...oh my...oh my... oh me,
a more pitiful creature I just couldn't
be."

Hartlie tried to cheer poor Wooly, trying hard
to make him smile but,
Wooly was determined all his life was toil and
trial.
"I'll walk you home," said Hartlie, hoping Wooly would
feel better,

but it started raining
gnats and frogs
making
Wooly's
spirits
wetter.

The lightening **flashed**, the thunder
crunched...

and all the Bog was frightened!

Wooly crawled up Hartlie's leg, his fears
now greatly heightened.

"It's just a little downpour,
don't you worry, don't you fret,"

Hartlie reassured his fuzzy friend,

who was now wringing wet.

They got to Wooly's
treehouse where
Hartlie built a fire,
to dry the little
wooly worm
and help them both
get dryer.

"Wooly... Now that it's so nice and warm in this cozy sitting room,
tell me why you see your life through eyes of doom and gloom,
"Oh...this is the way I've always been, life will never change for me,
I'm blighted by my silly looks and personality."
"Well surely you have something to be thankful for each day,
like love and life and friends and smiles and God to whom we pray."
"I guess that all is nice enough for those with everything,
but my creepy crawly low life isn't worth a single thing.

How would you   like to
wear a coat   that's fuzzy,
ot and brown,   that bits and pieces
stick to   making you the
local
clown."

Home is where the Hearth is

"Well...
Remember in the Bible, Joseph and his colorful coat?
Perhaps you should pretend that yours is also one of note.

It's all in how you view things,
your particular point of view
and yours needs some adjusting
and that only you can do.
But ...
if you want to change inside and get our Lord's
perspective,
then life will be much richer

and you'll start to be effective.
For life is how we see it,
we react to what we see,
if you think your life is harsh or dull,
that's exactly how it'll be.
But...
also on the other hand,
if you see it's good and kind,
then love and joy will bless your life
with smiles not far behind.

The gloom will lift and you will see,
from a different point fo view
that life is rich and wonderful,
making you a different you!"

"How can I change at this late date?"
Poor Wooly said in doubt,
"It seems too difficult for me...
I'm one without much clout."
"Without much clout?"
Said Hartlie, "Just how much clout is it you
need?

You can do all things
through Jesus Christ,
if you trust
and you believe!"

"D...do all things?!"
Wooly gasped, afraid to truly hope.
"Like change my point of view on life
so that I can learn to cope?"

"I know you can," said Hartlie,
"Just trust what Jesus said,
but remember that the range must start in
your heart
before your head."

"I can do it?
    ...I can do it

        ...I can do it!!!"

Wooly cried,
his heart now
pounding overtime
filling up with
joy inside
But his heart swelled up so big
and strong
that his coat began to tear,
"Better slow down,"
Hartlie cautioned

...but Wooly didn't
care.

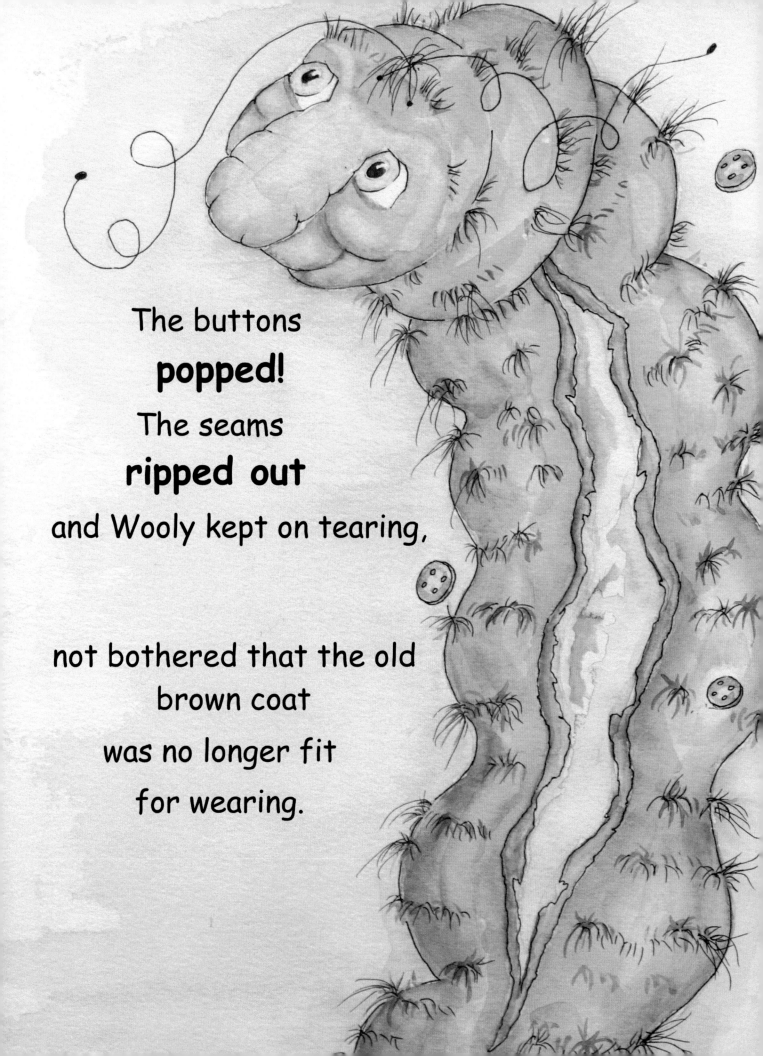

The buttons
popped!
The seams
ripped out
and Wooly kept on tearing,

not bothered that the old
brown coat
was no longer fit
for wearing.

Now Wooly stood on legs that felt decidedly
much lighter,
shook himself then,

danced around,
his future so
much brighter.

"Oh me...oh my!
I can't believe
just what it is
I'm seeing".

Hartlie blinked
his eyes
in disbelief
at Wooly's brand
new being.

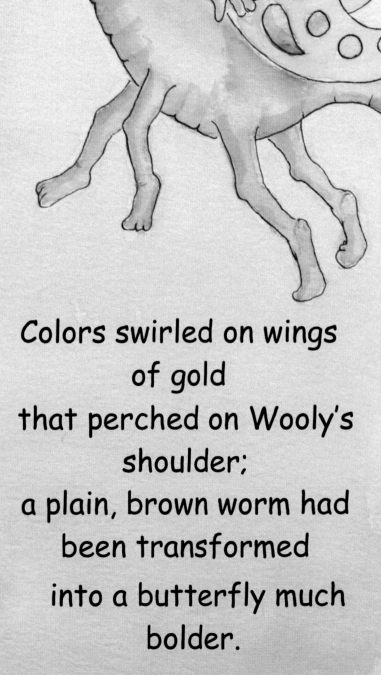

Colors swirled on wings
of gold
that perched on Wooly's
shoulder;
a plain, brown worm had
been transformed
into a butterfly much
bolder.

He fluttered over Hartlie's head and circled
ever higher,
"Come fly with me!!!"
He hollered as he soared right past
the fire.
"Oh I wish I could...
it looks like fun!
But I'm stuck here on the
ground.

I'll open up the door though,
there's no need your sticking
round."

Out the door and over the trees he fluttered
and he flew,
noticing how different things were
from his new point of view.
Free to see himself and life
as God would view it all,

for God made us all to soar
and fly,

instead of creep and crawl.

THE END... or could it be

THE BEGINNING

THE BEGINNING

Scriptures from the Holy Bible that help us understand who we are in God and how this affects every area of our lives.

Isaiah 40:29-31 He gives strength to the weary and increases the power of the weak. Even youths grow tired and weary and young men stumble and fall, but those who hope in the Lord will renew their strength. They will soar on wings like eagles; they will run and not grow weary, they will walk and not be faint.

Psalms 103:11 For as high as the heavens are above the Earth, so great is God's love for those who fear Him.

Mathew 6:26 "Look at the birds of the air, they do not sow or reap or store away in barns, and yet your Heavenly Father feeds them. Are you not much more valuable than they?"

1 Samuel 16:7 The Lord does not look at the things man looks at. Man looks at the outward appearance, but the Lord looks at the heart.

Jeremiah 29:11 "For I know the plans I have for you." Declares the Lord, "Plans to prosper you and not to harm you, Plans to give you hope and a future."

Psalm 34:18-19 The Lord is close to the brokenhearted and saves those who are crushed in spirit. A righteous man may have many troubles, but the Lord delivers him from them all.

This series was written in an effort
to help children understand that
no problem can overcome us
if we are walking close to Jesus,
trusting in His love and obeying
His commandments.

ISBN: 978-1-7370154-2-0

WWW.HARTLIE.COM

Made in the USA
Middletown, DE
25 June 2022

67792755R00018